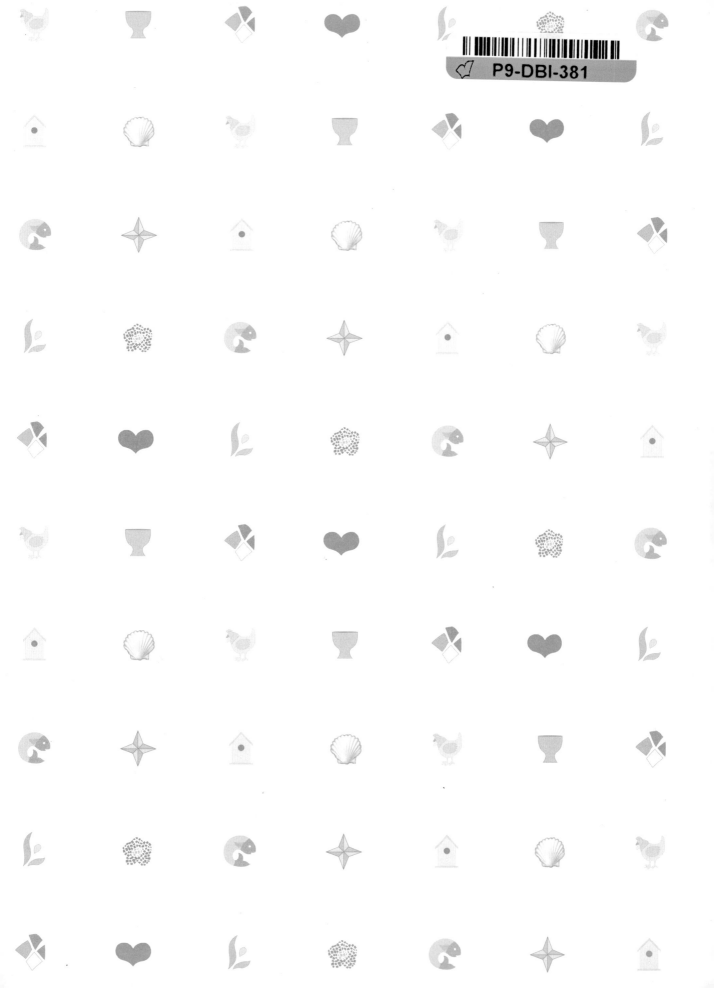

P9-DBI-381

Mosaics
made easy

Mosaics
made easy

Series Editors: Susan & Martin Penny

David & Charles

A DAVID & CHARLES BOOK

First published in the UK in 1999

Text and designs Copyright © David & Charles 1999
Photography and layout Copyright © David & Charles 1999

A catalogue record for this book is available from the British Library.

ISBN 0 7153 0890 4

Series Editors: Susan & Martin Penny
Designed and produced by Penny & Penny
Illustrations: Fred Fieber at Red Crayola
Photography: Jon Stone

Printed in Italy by LEGO SpA, Vicenza
for David & Charles
Brunel House Newton Abbot Devon

Contents

Introduction   6

Preparing Surfaces   8

Cutting, Fixing, Piecing   9

Grouting   13

Project   Summer Dining   14

Project   Eggshell Desk Set   22

Project   Magical Glass Vases   26

Project   Farmyard Placemats   30

Project   Seaside Mosaics   36

Project   Trug and Plant Holder   40

Project   Fabric-painted Mosaic Rug   44

Project   Fish and Shell Paper Mosaic   48

Project   Stylish Tray and Box   54

Project   Wood Mosaic Bird Tables   58

Acknowledgements   62

Suppliers   63

Index   64

Introduction to Mosaics

Mosaics Made Easy is a complete guide to the craft of mosaic work; many different types of material have been used to create projects including eggshells, sea shells, wood, tiles and broken china. For a quicker mosaic effect, paper pieces and paint have been used to make mosaic-style patterns on plates and a floor rug

Essential equipment

Below is a list of equipment needed for making mosaics:

- **Paper** – use copier paper to make a tracing of the design.
- **Soft pencil** – for marking design lines on to wood.
- **Chinagraph pencil** – for marking design lines on to shiny surfaces.
- **Decorator's paintbrush** – used for sealing wooden surfaces and applying varnish.
- **Paintbrush** – used for spreading ready-mixed tile adhesive and painting.
- **Kitchen paper** – for cleaning equipment.
- **Soft sponge** – to clean away excess grout.
- **Soft cloth** – for buffing after grouting.
- **Cutting knife** – used for cutting wooden mosaic shapes.
- **Mixing dish** – for mixing fix and grout.
- **Hammer** – for smashing china and tiles.
- **Rubber gloves** – to protect hands when using grout or cutting glass tiles.
- **Goggles** – to protect eyes when cutting tiles, or smashing china.
- **Cocktail stick** – used for cleaning dried grout from glass mosaic pieces.
- **Toothbrush** – used to clean dried grout from mosaic tiles and glass pieces.
- **Spatula** – used for spreading fix and grout.
- **Jam jars** – for separating mosaics pieces into different colours and shapes.
- **Tile nippers** – needed to cut glass tesserae tiles into shapes.

Fixatives and glues

Below is a list of products than can be used for attaching mosaic pieces. To help you decide which to use, consider the two surfaces you are trying to bond together and ask yourself, will the product you have chosen be strong enough to make the bond?

- **Tile fix** – a powder that is mixed with water to make a smooth thick paste, which should be spread with a spatula.
- **Fix and grout** – a powder, mixed and used in the same way as tile fix, but which can also be used for grouting.
- **Ready-mixed tile adhesive** – white glue-like substance, painted on the back of the mosaic pieces with a brush; use only when the working area is small.
- **PVA glue** – can be used when the mosaic pieces are lightweight, for example eggshells, plaster pieces or wooden shapes.
- **Silicone gel** – use for attaching glass or acrylic pieces to a glass or acrylic container; apply using a cocktail stick directly from the tube. Dries to a clear rubbery finish.
- **Wood glue** – use for attaching wooden mosaic shapes to wood or cardboard.
- **Découpage finisher** – for attaching paper pieces when making a mock mosaic.
- **Epoxy glue** – for attaching hard round objects, stones for example, to a vertical surface, when a quick bond is required.
- **Cement** – used for making mosaics outdoors using stones and shells.

Safety first

- Always wear goggles when cutting tiles or smashing china

- Break tiles and china under a tea-towel
- Grout can irritate your eyes and hands, so wear rubber gloves when using
- Silicone glue has a strong smell and can irritate your eyes and skin – work in a well ventilated room, and keep away from skin
- Broken china can have very sharp edges – so take care when handling it

Tips for preparing surfaces

- Rub down wood using fine sandpaper
- Surfaces must be clean before adding mosaic pieces
- Wash and dry china and glass to remove grease and dust

- Seal wooden surfaces using a PVA/water mix before adding mosaics
- Paint all surfaces not to be covered with mosaic pieces before beginning

Types of mosaics

Almost anything can be made into a mosaic as long as it has a flat side for bonding to the base. Below are some of the points to consider when choosing which material to work with.

- **Vitreous glass tesserae tiles**
  - Can be bought loose or glued to brown paper sheets, ready spaced for easier application. The paper backing is attached to the front of the tiles, and should only be removed after the tiles have been are fixed in place
  - Need to be cut using tile nippers
  - Wear protective goggles while cutting
  - Best applied to a firm wooden surface
  - Attach using fix, fix and grout; or for smaller designs, ready-mixed tile adhesive
- **Broken kitchen or bathroom wall tiles**
  - Break under a cloth using a hammer
  - No control over the shape of the pieces
  - Attach using fix, fix and grout; or for smaller designs, ready-mixed tile adhesive
- **Broken china**
  - Old broken china can be used
  - Break under a cloth using a hammer
  - No control over the shape of the pieces
  - Attach using fix, fix and grout; or for smaller designs, ready-mixed tile adhesive
- **Glass or acrylic shapes**
  - Produces a decorative jewel-like effect
  - Best when applied on to glass or acrylic
  - Attach using silicone glue
- **Plaster pieces**
  - Make your own shapes in the microwave
  - Cut to size using scissors
  - Mix your own colours
  - Attach using ready-mixed tile adhesive
- **Eggshells**
  - Make interesting 'leather look' effects
  - Wash to remove membrane and dirt
  - Use chicken, duck, goose or quail eggs
  - Protect finished surface with varnish
- **Wooden shapes**
  - Small pre-cut balsa-wood shapes available
  - Paint and apply to wood or card
  - Cut your own from balsa-wood

Preparing Surfaces

To ensure a good bond between the mosaic pieces and the base, the surface must be clean and free from dust, dirt and flaking paint. Rub down all wooden surfaces and coat with a sealer before applying the mosaic pieces. Transfer the design with or without a tracing, using a soft pencil directly on to the base board

Sealing before mosaics

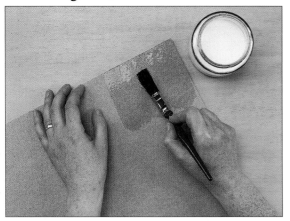

Seal MDF and wooden surfaces before gluing on mosaic pieces with a mix of one part PVA glue to three parts water. Leave to dry overnight, before adding the pieces.

Transferring the design

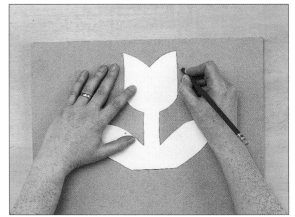

Make a tracing of the design on to white paper with a soft pencil. Cut out, then position on to the wood. Draw around the template, giving an outline for the mosaic.

Painting surfaces

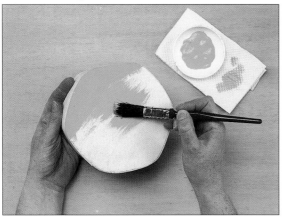

Sand, then paint with emulsion or acrylic all wooden project surfaces that will not be covered with mosaic pieces. Touch-up any marks after gluing on the mosaic pieces.

Designing freehand

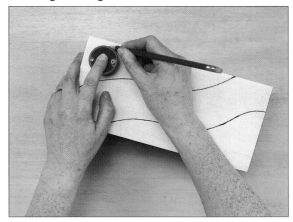

Using a soft pencil, draw freehand lines on to the wood, or use shapes like a bottle top to draw around. Keep the design simple, without angles, or it will be more difficult to fill.

Cutting, Fixing and Piecing

There are many different materials that can be used to create mosaics; and lots of ways of placing those pieces to create a variety of shapes and designs. China needs to be broken into small irregular pieces with a hammer; tiles need to be broken or nipped into regular shapes. After fixing on a base, the pieces need to be grouted

Using glass mosaic pieces

1 Apply silicone glue to the back of the glass pieces. Make sure the backs are completely covered or grout will seep under them and they will lose their transparency. Space 2-3mm ($^1/_{16}$-$^1/_8$in) apart, keeping them level, and push firmly in place.

2 Spread grout over the glass pieces, pushing it well down in the gaps. Wipe off the excess with a damp cloth, then use your finger to smooth the surface of the grout.

Using plaster pieces

1 Make a batter using plaster, colorant and warm water, then pour the mixture into a mould. Leave to dry for 1-1$^1/_2$ hours, then turn out on to kitchen paper. Heat in a microwave on low for 3 minutes; cool for 1 minute; microwave for 3 minutes. Leave to cool.

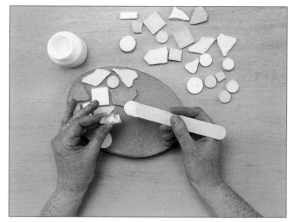

2 When dry, cut up the pieces into random sizes using scissors. Glue to the base, then seal pieces with acrylic sealer. Grout between, clean off marks, then varnish.

Cutting tiles

Always wear goggles when cutting glass tesserae or tile pieces as they may shatter causing splinters to fly off in all directions. Hold a tile on one edge between your finger and thumb. On the opposite edge, position the tile nipper quarter way across: nip sharply at this point and the tile will snap.

Fixing tiles

Attach the tiles using tile fix, or fix and grout. Mix the powder with water, and then spread a thick layer over the base; position the tiles, pushing them into the paste. Alternatively, position the tiles on the base, then lift them one at a time, 'buttering' the back with tile fix before replacing.

Paper-backed technique

1 Cut an area of paper-backed tiles the same shape as your base. Leaving the paper backing on, lay the tiles paper-side down on to your work surface, then carefully remove some of the tiles, making a pattern. Spread a 3mm (1/8in) thick layer of tile fix, fix and grout or ready-mixed tile adhesive on the base, then attach the tiles to the base, paper-side up.

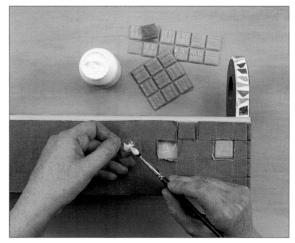

2 Using a craft knife, cut away the brown paper in front of the spaces, where you have removed tiles. Spread adhesive thickly on the back of a different coloured tile then position it in a space. Continue adding tiles until all the holes are full. Dampen the brown paper, then peel off before grouting.

Using paper pieces

1 Cut giftwrap and wallpaper into random shapes. Draw the design on to the plate using a chinagraph pencil. Position the paper pieces on the plate, leaving 3mm (1/8in) between the pieces. Starting in the middle of your design, lift the pieces one at a time, then glue back in position using découpage finisher. Smooth out bubbles, then wipe away any excess glue.

2 Paint a coat of découpage finisher over the surface of the plate, then leave to dry. To give the mosaic a three-dimensional look, coat each paper piece with dimensional finisher: run the finisher around the outside, then fill the centre, allowing the liquid to flow out to the edges.

Using broken china

1 Place the unbroken china or tiles inside a strong paper bag or folded newspaper. Wearing goggles, hit the china hard using the metal edge of a hammer head, breaking it into small pieces. Check the size of the pieces, and then if necessary repeat the process. Sort the pieces into storage jars, removing any that have crumbled or are badly broken.

2 For a large design area use tile fix or fix and grout to attach the china pieces; for smaller projects, spread a ready-mixed tile adhesive on to the base, and then 'butter' the underside of the pieces, before pressing them into place. Remove any excess adhesive, then leave to dry before grouting.

Using eggshells

Wash and dry the eggshells. Dab a small amount of PVA glue within the cut out area of a stencil. Break off a fingernail size piece of eggshell and place on to the glue. Press the eggshell with a finger to break it, then using the tip of a craft knife, slide the eggshell fragments apart. When dry, varnish.

Making mock mosaic tiles

Use double-sided foam stickers to make stamps that resemble mosaic tiles. Cut the stickers into square pads; remove the covering from one side and attach the pads to a block of wood or cardboard. Remove the protective covering from the other side, apply coloured paint to each pad, then stamp.

Using stones

Glue aquarium stones in place using two-part epoxy glue. Once mixed, the glue will remain tacky for a very short time. Spread the glue on to the base; then use a lolly stick to push the stones in place, leaving approximately (3mm) $\frac{1}{8}$in between the stones. When dry, grout between the stones.

Using wooden shapes

Paint mosaic balsa-wood shapes with two coats of acrylic paint. When dry, use PVA glue to attach them to the base. Seal the surface of the shapes with a coat of clear varnish or sealer. Grout between the shapes, then wipe away any excess grout. Sand off any marks, retouch the paint, then varnish.

Grouting

Grout is a paste made when grouting powder is mixed with water; the powder can be bought in white or black and can be tinted with a powder or liquid colorant. The paste is used to fill the gaps between the mosaic pieces, to give an unbroken surface, while forming a strong bond between the pieces and the base

Mixing and tinting grout

Add water to the grout powder, mixing thoroughly to make a smooth paste. If you are using a powder colorant, add it before the water; if you are using liquid, add it after.

Applying grout

Always wear rubber gloves while grouting as it can irritate your skin and eyes. Spread using a rubber spatula, lolly stick or your finger, pushing it well into the spaces.

Cleaning away excess grout

Before the grout dries, wipe over the surface of the mosaic pieces with a damp sponge, several times. Keep rinsing the sponge until the excess grout has been removed.

Buffing grout to a shine

When nearly dry, buff the surface of the mosaic pieces with a soft cloth to remove any residue. Allow to dry completely before buffing the pieces again to make them shine.

Summer Dining

When the sun shines and the sky is blue, there can be no nicer way to enjoy the summer weather than by dining outside. Whether you are having breakfast or a picnic, this pretty yet durable table top will make the simplest meal look like a gourmet feast

This design can be adapted to suit any size and shape of table; for a large dining table, add more flower pots and extend the border; for a smaller table use just one or two pots.

You will need
- MDF 12mm x 46x61cm (½in x 18x24in) – or cut to the size of your table top
- Terracotta pot
- Vitreous glass tesserae tiles – 150 deep blue, 70 yellow, 70 orange, 60 dark green, 70 lime green, 120 light blue, 230 shaded blues
- Fix and grout 2.5kg (5½lb) – white
- PVA glue
- Emulsion paint – white, blue
- Tile nippers, paintbrush
- Pencil, ruler, white paper, scissors
- Small scraper, lolly stick
- Sponge, spatula, decorator's paintbrush
- Mixing bowl, water, small rolling pin
- Sheet, newspaper, goggles, rubber gloves

Tracing the design
1 Trace over the flower motifs, and the flower pot on pages 19, 20 and 21 on to white paper with a soft pencil. Cut out the flower templates and three flower pot shapes.

2 Mark the centre point of the table, then place the flower pot and the flower head tracings evenly across the table top, positioning the centre point of the sunflower over the centre of the table. Draw around the templates: this will give an outline for your mosaic pieces.

Preparing your working area
1 Cover your work table or floor with an old sheet or newspaper.

2 Some mosaic tiles are glued to a paper backing sheet: these will need to be soaked in water for a few minutes to remove the paper.

3 Always wear protective goggles when cutting glass tesserae pieces as they may shatter causing splinters to fly off in all directions. Mosaic pieces can be very difficult to cut accurately; they will nearly always break if there is a fault line. Save all the broken pieces as even the smallest sliver can be used to fill in a gap. To cut in half: hold the piece on one edge between your finger and thumb. On the opposite edge position the tile nipper, quarter of the way across the tile. Nip the tile

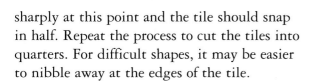

sharply at this point and the tile should snap in half. Repeat the process to cut the tiles into quarters. For difficult shapes, it may be easier to nibble away at the edges of the tile.

4 Seal the MDF table top with a mix of one part PVA glue and three parts water; leave to dry overnight. This will stop the fix and grout soaking into the wood.

5 Paint the underside and the edges of the MDF with two coats of white emulsion, then leave to dry.

Creating your design

1 All the tiles should be cut and positioned on to the table top before attempting to fix them in place. This will give you the opportunity to make any adjustments to your design.

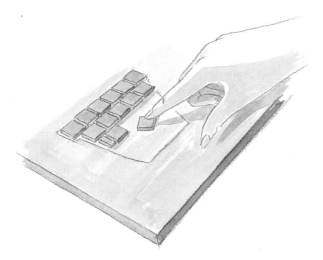

2 Arrange the full sized orange and lime green tiles in different patterns within the flower pot areas of the design. Cut tiles with the nippers to fill the spaces.

Working the tulip

1 Cut deep blue and yellow tiles into small pieces. Nip the tile in half then half again

to form squares: don't worry if your shapes are irregular as the grout will fill any gaps. Arrange the tile pieces within the flower head: place whole, dark green tiles in the leaf and stalk areas of the design, then infill with smaller pieces of dark and lime green.

Working the daisy

1 Cut enough deep blue tiles into quarters to cover the majority of the petal area, then add several pieces of yellow to the centre of the flower. Cover the leaf and stalk areas with dark and lime green tiles.

Working the sunflower

1 Arrange whole yellow tiles inside the sunflower and fill the spaces with smaller pieces cut to size. Add pieces of orange and blue to form the centre. Use dark green tiles for the stalk.

Mixing the fix and grout

1 Tip a small amount of fix and grout powder into an old bowl: it is easier to make up small amounts, as the grout will soon get dry and unworkable.

2 Add water, a little at a time, until you have a smooth thick paste. Stir until all the powder is mixed into the water and the paste is lump free. Scrape the bowl between mixes and clean thoroughly after you have finished, or the grout will set hard in the bowl.

Applying the mosaics

1 After the tiles have been arranged on to the base, they can be fixed to the MDF using one of the following techniques.

Method 1
Tiles can be lifted, one at a time, 'buttered' on the underside with mortar, then pressed back into place. This is time consuming, but it means you can lift the tiles individually

without having to clear the whole mosaic.

Method 2

Starting at the centre of the design, remove the tiles carefully, laying them out in the same position as they were on the board. Spread a layer of paste, approximately 6mm (¼in) thick over a small area of the design, then replace the tile pieces one at a time, pressing lightly into the mortar.

2 Starting with the central flower pot, fix the tiles to the base board using the method you prefer (see above). Repeat with the other two flower pots. It can be difficult to keep the small tiles pieces level: a small rolling pin, very gently rolled over the area, will ensure that all the pieces are level. Remove any mortar that is forced up between the tiles as you roll. As you

complete each area, scrape away the excess mortar, then wipe over with a damp cloth before it dries.

Completing the design

1 When you have finished fixing the flower pots, the border edge can be completed using alternate dark blue and light blue tiles.

2 Finish the design by filling in the background area using assorted light blue tiles, fixing the complete tiles before infilling with the smaller pieces. Allow to dry for a few days before grouting.

Grouting your design

1 Mix water with the fix and grout, making a smooth paste, slightly runnier than before.

2 Apply the grout with a rubber spatula or damp sponge, spreading it over the surface of the table, and pushing it into the spaces between the tiles, completing an area of approximately 20cm (8in) at a time. Use the spatula to remove the excess grout from the surface of the tiles, then wipe over with a clean damp sponge several times.

3 When nearly dry buff the surface of the tiles to remove any grout and reveal the bright colours of the tiles.

4 Allow to dry completely for two or three days before buffing the tiles again to make them shine.

5 If the fix and grout has marked the painted edge of the table top, rub down lightly with sandpaper before touching up the sides using white emulsion paint.

Decorating the flower pot

1 Measure the circumference around the top rim of the flower pot, then on your work surface arrange enough dark blue tiles diagonally to cover the required length.

2 Using the tile nipper, cut small pieces of lime green, yellow and orange tile. Arrange the pieces on your work surface between the whole blue tiles, filling the spaces.

3 Mix the fix and grout as before. Lay the pot over at an angle, propping it so that you can work on one quarter of the design at a time. Spread a 6mm ($\frac{1}{4}$in) layer on to the top rim of the flower pot.

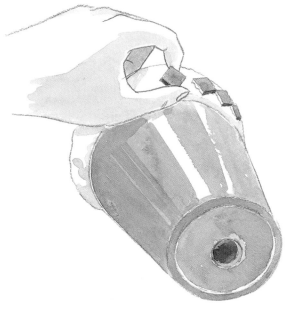

4 Press the dark blue tiles in place, then infill with smaller pieces; clean off any surplus fix and grout. Repeat for the other three quarters. Leave to dry.

5 Mix the fix and grout powder, to a smooth paste as before. Wearing rubber gloves, spread the mix over the top of the flower pot, pushing the grout well into the gaps between the tiles with your fingers.

6 Wipe over with a clean piece of damp sponge several times. When nearly dry, buff the tiles to a shine.

7 Apply two coats of coloured emulsion paint to the bottom of the flower pot. If they are to be used outside, seal the surface with varnish.

Daisy

Sunflower

Flower pot for the sunflower,
daisy and tulip

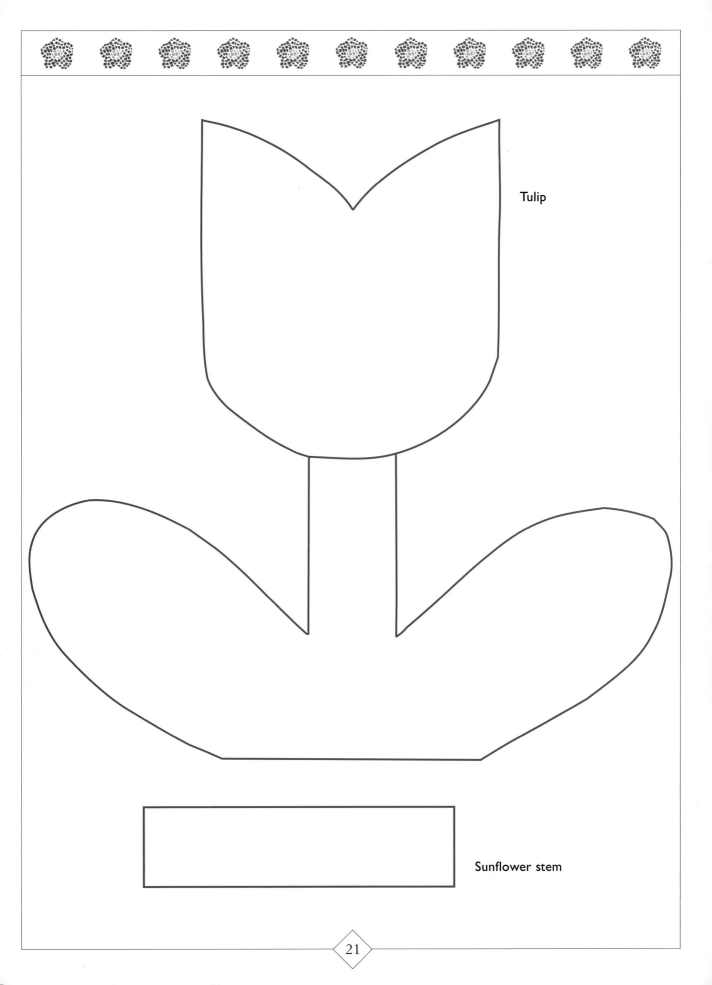

Tulip

Sunflower stem

Eggshell Desk Set

Broken eggshells have been used to create the crazed leather look on this cardboard desk set. The brown background is made from chicken's eggs, while the decorative motifs are worked in duck and goose eggs; seal the surface with varnish for a water resistant finish

You will need

- Plain cardboard desk set
- Eggs – pale brown, pale blue and white
- Thick paper, tracing paper, pencil, scissors
- Craft knife, cutting mat
- PVA glue, small and medium paintbrush
- Water-based satin varnish
- Blu-tack

Preparing the eggshells

1 Crack the eggs and keep the contents for cooking. Carefully peel away the membrane from inside the shells, then wash and dry thoroughly. Almost all eggshells are suitable for mosaic work: chicken, duck, goose and quail, which should be available at most good food shops.

2 If you prefer to use brighter shades, the unbroken eggshells can be painted with two or three coats of acrylic paint. Allow to dry thoroughly before continuing.

Cutting the stencil

1 Trace over the designs on page 25, using tracing paper. Lay the tracing on to card and then draw over the design lines transferring the motifs to the card. Lay the card on to a cutting mat, then, using a sharp craft knife, cut out the shapes.

Applying the design

1 Position the card template on to one side of the letter rack, holding it in place with blu-tack. Dab a small amount of glue within the cut out area of the stencil: only work on a very small area as PVA glue dries very quickly.

2 Break off a fingernail size piece of pale blue or white eggshell and place down on to the glued area.

3 Press the eggshell with a finger to break it into smaller pieces. Work quickly before the glue dries.

4 Using the tip of a craft knife, slide the eggshell fragments apart. This will give the impression of mosaic pieces.

5 Repeat the design on the opposite end of the letter rack by reversing the stencil and filling with broken eggshells as before.

6 Centre the stencil design on to the front of the letter rack. Apply glue to the cut out areas. Work on a single leaf at a time as the glue dries very quickly. Reposition the stencil over the worked area and continue filling in the design.

7 When you have completed the motifs on the front and sides of the letter rack, fill in the background area with pale brown shells.

Notepad and pencil pot

1 Position the cardboard template over the front of the notepad.

2 Apply glue to a small area within the template. Press a small piece of eggshell on top of the glue, breaking it into small pieces.

3 Using a craft knife, carefully slide the pieces apart while the glue is still wet. Repeat for the pencil pot.

Applying the varnish

1 Once the glue behind the eggshells is dry, use a medium brush to apply five coats of varnish over the eggshells for protection. Allow to dry for about two hours between each coat.

Motif for the notepad.

Motif for the pencil holder
and the ends of the letter rack.

Motif for the front of the letter rack.

Magical Glass Vases

These stunning vases should be stood in front of a light or window to make them shine. Use all year round to display flowers, or at Christmas time as a decoration. If the container is made from glass, a candle can be placed inside, allowing the light to create a magical effect

You will need

- Glass or acrylic vases
- Glass or acrylic mosaic shapes
- Glass or acrylic mosaic beads
- Silicone gel
- Grout – black
- Soft cloth, sponge
- Water, rubber gloves
- Old toothbrush, cocktail stick
- Container for mixing grout, spatula

Preparing the vase

1 Wash the containers thoroughly to remove any grease and dust; allow to dry completely. This project can be worked using glass or acrylic containers, as the silicone glue will work well on both surfaces.

Choosing your design

1 Separate the mosaic pieces into different shapes and colours.

2 If you are making a repeat pattern, measure the container and plan the design on paper to ensure that you have enough mosaic pieces to finish the design.

Piecing the green vase

1 Coat the back of a mosaic piece with silicone glue. Make sure the back is completely covered with silicone, or grout will seep under the shape once it is stuck in place, and so lose its transparency. Silicone can be very difficult to remove, so do not get it on the front of the pieces or on to your hands. It may be easier to apply the silicone using a cocktail stick.

2 Arrange the pieces, one at a time, on to the container, leaving spaces of about 2-3mm (^{1}/16-^{1}/8in) between each piece. Push the pieces well in place, keeping them level with the container.

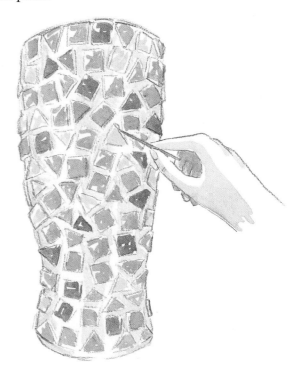

3 Starting at the top of the vase, arrange a row of triangular shaped pieces around the rim, with points facing downwards. Keep the pieces close to the top, as this will make it easier to grout the top of the container. Below this place another row of triangles, the other way up, between the points.

4 Under the triangles, add three rows of square pieces, spacing them evenly around the container. Repeat the triangular pattern and the rows of square pieces as many times as needed to cover the vase. The same spacing applies at the bottom as at the top: take the pieces right down to the base of the container. Allow to dry overnight before grouting.

Piecing the goblet vase

1 Attach a row of the orange circular shapes around the rim of the container in the same way as before. Below this fix a row of red tear-drop shapes.

2 Fill the remainder of the surface with an assortment of red and orange pieces.

Continue with the pattern or apply a random design until the vase is covered. Allow to dry overnight before grouting.

Piecing the tall vase

1 Using a variety of shapes and colours apply the mosaic pieces randomly over the vase. When the whole area is covered, allow to dry overnight before grouting.

Cleaning away the silicone

1 Although the silicone may seem dry enough to grout within a few hours, leave it overnight to ensure the pieces are stuck firmly in place.

2 Using a cocktail stick, carefully clean away any dried silicone that has been squeezed out between the pieces.

Grouting the vases

1 The grout can be irritating to the eyes and skin, so it is advisable to wear rubber gloves while grouting.

2 Mix the black grout powder with water: add a spoonful at a time, until it forms a fairly stiff paste. Apply over the mosaic pieces, using your fingers to push it into the spaces. Wipe away any excess grout, then smooth between the pieces paying particular attention to the top and bottom edges of the container. Allow the grout to harden for approximately 10 minutes before continuing.

3 Once the grout has hardened a little, use a damp sponge to wipe over the pieces, one at a time. Do not let the sponge come into contact with the grout or it may get wiped away.

Use these jewelled vases to display flowers, or to hold candles at Christmas time.

4 Once the grout has set overnight, use a soft toothbrush to gently brush away any hardened grout stuck to the front of the shapes; to clean the edges, use the sharp end of a cocktail stick.

5 Finally, buff up the mosaic shapes using a soft cloth to make them shine.

6 If the vases get dusty, use a damp cloth to wipe over the surface.

Farmyard Placemats

If you would like to try mosaics, but feel nervous about smashing up china or breaking tiles, then this is a project that will surely appeal. The pieces are made in a mould from a plaster resin, and then dried slowly in the microwave. Use a pre-shaped mould or any shallow microwave dish to make the pieces

You will need
- Cork placemats – 30x23cm (12x9in)
- Cork coasters – 11x11cm (4x4in)
- Plaster powder for mosaics
- Grout colorant – brown, yellow, duck egg blue, red, pale blue, dusty pink, grey
- Pre-shaped plaster mosaic mould or shallow microwave dish
- Plastic beaker, warm water
- Tracing paper, pencil, chinagraph pencil
- Ready-mixed tile adhesive
- Acrylic sealer
- Tablespoon, scissors
- Sponge, rubber gloves

Tracing the design

1 Using the templates on pages 34 and 35, make a tracing of the chicken and duck designs. Cut out the shapes and place them centrally on the top of the placemats. Draw around the outline using a chinagraph pencil.

2 Follow the same procedure for the flower tracing on page 33, placing a flower in each corner of the mat.

3 For the coaster: place the flower tracing in the centre, then draw around the outline with a chinagraph pencil.

Making the pieces

1 Put approximately 2 tablespoons of plaster mix in a plastic beaker. Add a squirt of colorant to the powder: the more colorant you add, the deeper the colour will be. Remember when mixing colours that the plaster will be a slightly lighter shade when dry. Add enough warm water to make the consistency of pancake batter, stirring vigorously as you go to remove any lumps.

2 Pour the mixture slowly into a mould, but do not fill completely to the top. You can use a pre-shaped mosaic mould, which can be bought with the plaster mix; or use a shallow microwave dish. Tap the mould lightly underneath to remove any air bubbles. Try to

keep the surface level: the smoother the surface, the easier it will be to achieve a flat finish on your mat.

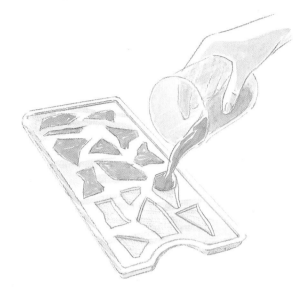

3 Leave the pieces to dry in the mould or dish for 1-1½ hours. The plaster should be dry to the touch but will still be damp underneath.

4 Turn the mould or dish out on to a piece of kitchen paper. If you have used a large dish, gently press around the edges then turn it over to release the plaster.

5 Place the plaster pieces on to kitchen paper and place in a microwave. Set the microwave on a low or defrost setting; never

use a medium or high setting. Do not microwave the plastic mould tray. Microwave for 3 minutes; cool for 1 minute; microwave for 3 minutes. Leave until cool to the touch. Alternatively, dry naturally overnight.

6 When dry, use the pieces as they are; or cut up into random sizes using scissors. Do not leave the pieces too large or they will be difficult to arrange.

7 Make a quantity of the colours needed for the design. Try to remember how much colorant you added to the powder, so that each batch will be roughly the same colour. As you produce the pieces place them on the design, so that quantities can be judged. Any variations in shade can be mixed up within the design. You will need more background pieces than any other, i.e. yellow and duck egg blue. Make orange pieces by mixing red and yellow colorant with the plaster, and a little red to the brown to give a rusty brown for the chicken's body.

Chicken placemat

1 Use rusty brown pieces for the chicken's body, with dark brown to accent the wings; orange for the feet and beak; red for the comb; dusty pink for the flower centres, and blue or dusty pink for the petals. The immediate area around the chicken is filled with yellow, and

the remainder of the placemat covered in duck egg blue.

2 When applying the pieces, work on a single area of the design at any one time. Apply a thin layer of ready-mixed tile adhesive to the back of a mosaic piece, and a small amount to the placemat. Press the pasted mosaic piece in place, keeping it level. Leave a small gap between each piece, with a slightly larger space around the edges of the birds and flowers for definition. Leave to dry completely.

Duck placemat

1 The duck's body is filled with grey mosaic, with a line of blue pieces to define the wings; the beak and feet are orange; use a tiny piece of dark brown for the eye; yellow for the flower centres, and dusty pink or blue for the petals.

Coaster

1 Arrange blue or dusty pink mosaic pieces over the flower design, using a different colour for each centre. Finish the background area of the design with yellow or duck egg blue. If you have made excess coloured pieces for the placemats, you can use them up when making the flowers. Because of the small area that you are covering, do not worry if the pieces are not exactly within the design area.

Grouting your design

1 Leave the mats to dry overnight. Mix water with the grouting powder, until the consistency of oatmeal is achieved.

2 Wearing rubber gloves, use your fingers to spread grout over the surface of the mat. Clean off surplus grout with a knife and then wipe with a damp sponge.

3 When dry, polish off any remaining dry grout with a soft cloth to reveal the true colours of the mosaic pieces.

Sealing the mats

1 Seal the surface of the mats and coasters with several coats of acrylic sealer. Allow to dry completely between each coat, and before using the mats.

Use the flower tracing below to transfer the outlines to the coaster.

Make a tracing from this duck design to transfer the outlines to the placemat.

Make a tracing from the chicken design above to
transfer the outlines to the placemat.

Seaside Mosaics

Shells can be used in place of cobblestones to make a step; they can be set into a patio or used as a decorative area in the rockery. If you prefer something on a smaller scale, cover a ceramic lamp base with aquarium stones, adding a shade decorated with sea shells

If you would like to make the seaside mosaic into a conservatory table top, cut MDF to size, and seal the top with a thin glue/water mix before attaching the shells and stones using two-part epoxy glue.

You will need
- Shells
- Flat shiny stones
- Aquarium gravel – multi-coloured
- Ceramic lamp base
- Ready-mixed cement
- Hard-core – broken bricks or small stones
- Two-part epoxy glue, lolly stick, spatula
- Tile grout, rubber gloves
- White paper, pencil, chinagraph pencil
- Masking tape, bowl of water, sponge
- Mixing board and trowel

Planning your design

1 Cut a piece of white paper the size you would like your shell mosaic to be. Wash the shells, stones and aquarium stones in warm soapy water and dry thoroughly. Position the paper close to where you will be making the mosaic. Place the shells and stones on to the paper, roughly following the photograph on page 38, or using your own arrangement.

Preparing the step

1 Clear a rectangle of garden just larger than the size of the paper. Remove the soil to a depth of 7.5cm (3in). Then back-fill the hole to a depth of 5cm (2in) with hard-core made from broken bricks and small stones.

2 Tip a quantity of ready-mixed cement on to a mixing board. Add water and mix, following the manufacturer's instructions.

3 Trowel the cement into the hole, covering the hard-core and making the level just higher than the surrounding garden – this will allow for shrinkage whilst drying.

Laying the step

1 While the cement is still wet, mark out the design roughly using a stick.

2 Remove the shells one at a time from the paper and press them into the cement. Push

the larger objects in deeper to keep the surface level. Repeat with the flat shiny stones and finally the aquarium stones.

3 Leave the cement to set for several days, before replacing the earth or sand up to and slightly over the edges of the cement.

Preparing the lamp

1 Remove the electrical fitting and cable from the lamp base.

2 Wipe the lamp base with a damp cloth to remove dust and greasy marks.

Transferring the design

1 Trace over the fish design opposite on to white paper with a soft pencil. You can use a photocopier if you need to enlarge or reduce the size of the fish to fit the lamp. Cut out the fish, then, using masking tape, attach the tracing to the lamp.

2 Draw around the fish tracing using a chinagraph pencil.

Applying the stones

1 Sort the aquarium stones by colour into jam jars; choose flat stones that are of a regular shape and roughly the same size.

2 The stones should be applied to the surface of the lamp using two-part epoxy glue. Once mixed, the glue will remain tacky for a very short time, so work quickly and with very small quantities, following the manufacturer's instructions.

3 Spread a small amount of two-part epoxy glue on to the fish area of the lamp base, then apply light coloured stones to the glue. Use a lolly stick to push the stones in place, leaving approximately 3mm (1/8in) between the stones for the grout. Use a different coloured stone for the eye and the mouth.

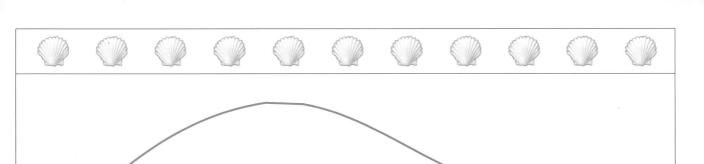

Make a tracing of this fish motif to transfer the outlines on to the lamp base.

4 Fill in the background area in the same way, using the darker coloured stones to give a mottled effect.

Grouting the lamp base

1 Wearing rubber gloves, slowly add water to a small amount of grouting powder until you have a thick, smooth paste: an approximate ratio of three parts grout to one part water.

2 Spread the grout on to the stones, using a lolly stick, spatula, or your fingers, pushing the grout well into the spaces between the stones. Leave the grout to set for about 10-15 minutes, then using a wet sponge, wipe away the excess. Keep rinsing the sponge in clean water and wiping off the grout until all the stones are clean.

3 Once dry, polish away any remaining powder on the stones with a soft cloth.

4 Replace the electrical fitting, before adding a lampshade decorated with sea shells.

Trug and Plant Holder

Brighten your home with this cheerful mosaic trug, finished using
paper-backed tiles. Put it on your kitchen window sill and fill with pots
of herbs, then you will always have fresh parsley, basil or coriander
easily to hand, to add to your cooking

You will need

- Wooden trug
- Wooden flower pot holder
- Vitreous glass tesserae tiles, paper-backed –
  bright blue, dark blue, yellow, dark green,
  lime green, orange
- Ceramic tiles and broken china
- Glass half-domed beads
- Wooden birdhouse shapes
- Wood primer
- Emulsion or acrylic paint – green, blue, yellow,
  terracotta, brown
- Fix and grout or ready-mixed tile adhesive –
  white
- PVA glue
- Clear polyurethane varnish, gloss
- Tile nippers, small scraper, craft knife
- Squared paper, coloured pencil
- Piece of sponge, spatula, decorator's paintbrush
- Mixing bowl, water, goggles, rubber gloves

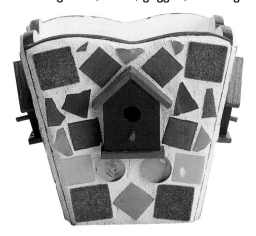

Planning the trug design

1 Plan your design on squared paper using
coloured pencils showing where the coloured
tiles will be positioned. Lay the bright blue
paper-backed tiles that you will be using for the
background of your design on to one side of the
trug. Cut the tiles to fit, leaving the backing
paper on, and the tiles in one sheet (see
Cutting, Fixing and Piecing, page 10). Prepare
another sheet for the other side of the trug.

2 Lay the sheet of background tiles paper-side
down, on your work surface. Carefully
remove tiles where the other coloured tiles are
to be fixed, following your plan.

Preparing the trug

1 Smooth down any rough surfaces on your
trug with sandpaper, before applying one
coat of wood primer.

2 Drill holes in the bottom of the trug to
allow the water to drain away, or buy a
plant tray to fit into the bottom of the trug.

3 Using emulsion or acrylic, paint the trug
inside and out with two coats, excluding
the areas that will be covered by the mosaic.

Sealing the surfaces

1 Seal the painted areas with two coats of
polyurethane varnish, then seal the

remaining unpainted areas to be covered with mosaic pieces with a mix of one part PVA to three parts water (see Preparing Surfaces, page 8). Leave the trug to dry overnight.

Applying the mosaics

1 Tip a small amount of fix and grout powder into an old bowl, then add water a little at a time until you have a smooth thick paste; stir until the paste is lump free.

2 Lay the trug on its side, then spread with a layer of paste approximately 3mm (⅛in) thick; or for small projects, use ready-mixed tile adhesive on the back of the tiles. Lay the tiles paper-side-up on to the pasted trug, then press well down into the paste.

3 Use a sharp craft knife to cut away the paper in front of the spaces where you have removed a tile.

4 Following the colour plan, fix the tiles into the empty spaces on the side of the trug. 'Butter' the underside of each tile piece with paste or adhesive before pressing it into place. Repeat for the other side of the trug. Leave the glue to dry overnight.

5 Wet the brown paper covering the tiles on the front and back of the trug with a sponge: the paper should peel away. Use more water if any paper remains on the tiles.

6 Decorate the handles with pieces of broken tile. Always wear protective goggles when cutting glass tesserae pieces as they may shatter causing splinters to fly off in all directions. To cut a tile: hold the tile on one edge between your finger and thumb. On the opposite edge position the tile nipper quarter of the way across: nip the tile sharply at this point and it should snap. Repeat the process to make smaller pieces. Mosaic pieces can be very difficult to cut accurately as they will nearly always break on a fault line; keep the small pieces as they can be very useful on places like the handles.

Decorating the flower pot

1 Smooth down any rough surfaces on your pot with sandpaper before applying one coat of wood primer; leave to dry.

2 Drill holes in the bottom of the pot to allow the water to drain away.

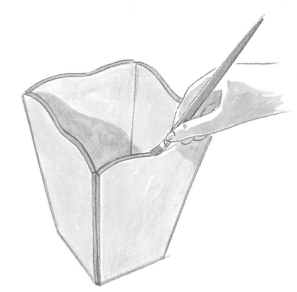

3 Paint the top edge, angles and inside the pot with two or three coats of emulsion or acrylic. Paint the wooden shapes that will be

used to decorate the front of the pot in the same way. When dry, seal the paint with a coat of polyurethane varnish.

4 Seal the sides of the pot, with the PVA/water mix used for the trug; leave to dry.

5 Cover the sides of the pot with whole and broken tiles, broken china, glass-domed beads, and painted wooden shapes. 'Butter' the underside of the pieces with paste or adhesive before pressing them into place.

Grouting your designs

1 Add water to the fix and grout or grout powder, making a smooth paste.

2 Apply the grout with a rubber spatula or your fingers, pushing it into the spaces between the tiles. Run your thumb around the angles of the pot and the trug handles to make a neat smooth edge, then use a spatula to take away excess grout. Before the grout dries, wipe over the mosaic pieces carefully, using a damp sponge, several times.

3 When nearly dry, buff the surface of the mosaic pieces to remove any residue. Allow to dry completely before buffing the pieces again to make them shine. If the grout has marked the painted edges of the pot and the trug: wipe over with a damp cloth, then repaint and varnish the marked areas.

Fabric-Painted Mosaic Rug

This welcoming half-moon shaped rug has been cleverly stamped to look like mosaic tiles. Easy to complete in just a few evenings, the technique can also be used on a larger piece of canvas to create a mock 'mosaic floor' covering in place of the real thing

You will need

- Semi-circular smooth weave canvas rug 90x46cm (36x18in)
- Acrylic paint – white, lemon, fuschia, pale blue, powder blue, duck egg blue, turquoise
- Double-sided self adhesive foam stickers – 12x25mm (½x1in)
- Stiff thick cardboard
- Scissors, pencil, ruler, card
- Tracing paper, white paper
- Block of wood – 4.5x4.5cm (1¾x1¾in) and 3.5x3.5cm (1¼x1¼in)
- Paintbrushes, PVA glue
- Flat dish for mixing paint, water, kitchen paper

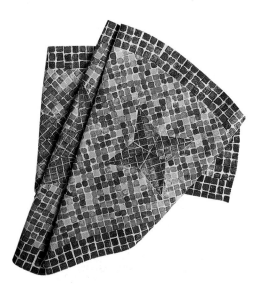

Tracing the design

1 Using the template on page 47, trace over the two large triangular shapes that form the point of the star.

2 Lay the tracing on cardboard, then draw over the triangles, transferring the design lines; cut out the triangles. These two triangles, placed side by side, form one of the eight points of the large star; see the photograph opposite, and the diagram below.

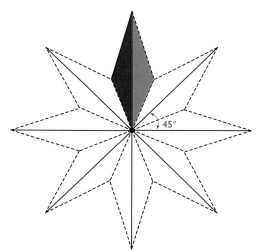

3 On a sheet of white paper, draw an eight point star with 45° angles. Place the cardboard triangles either side of one of the drawn lines; draw around the outside edge. Repeat for the other lines making an eight point star. Cut out the star. The finished size of the large star will be 28cm (11in).

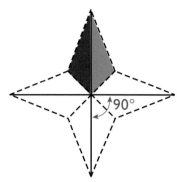

Draw a four-pointed star with 90° angles, and then use it to build a star for transferring the design lines on to the canvas.

4 Make the smaller star in the same way: a four-pointed star with 90° angles. Cut out the two smaller triangular shapes from cardboard, then use them to draw the star shape above on to white paper; cut out the star. The finished size of the star is 15cm (6in).

Arranging your design

1 Lay the large paper star template in the centre of the rug. Draw around it lightly using a soft pencil. Remove the paper template and draw lines from each point to the centre, dividing the points into triangles. This will help to guide you when placing the stamp. Transfer the small star in the same way, placing one on either side of the central star.

Making the mosaic stamps

1 Take the two triangles of card that you used to make the eight point star, and trace around them both on to a piece of thick cardboard. You should have two halves that mirror each other – one left facing and the other right facing.

2 Cut the self-adhesive foam stickers into 12mm (¹/₂in) squares. Remove the adhesive backing paper from one side, then fix on to the drawn cardboard triangles. Leave a small gap between each sticker to give the impression of mosaic pieces, and allow the stickers to overlap the edges. Cut through the cardboard and the stickers, following the pencil lines that you can see between the stickers: you will have two

triangular shaped stamps. Make the stamps for the four-pointed star in the same way.

3 To make it easier to hold when stamping, glue several layers of cardboard on to the back of each triangle.

Applying the paint

1 Mix together fuschia and powder blue paint in a flat dish to make a deep lilac colour.

2 Remove the adhesive covering papers from the face of the foam stickers on the stamp. Using a brush, apply a coat of lilac paint to each of the foam shapes. Make sure that any excess paint is removed from between the squares. Prime the stamp by applying it to a spare piece of fabric, after a couple of applications the paint will adhere to the sticker much better. You may need to cut several stamps if you decide to print more than two stars, as with continuous use, the paint will build up on the stamp, giving a fuzzy outline.

3 Once you feel confident you can apply paint to your rug. Brush lilac paint on to the foam shapes on the stamp; reapplying the paint between each application. Place the inside edge of the triangle along the right-hand side of the top pencil line on the rug. Apply even pressure over the whole of the stamp, then lift off carefully. Reapply the paint and continue

around the star applying the stamp to the right-hand side of each point.

4 To complete the star, repeat the process with the left-hand stamp using fuschia pink. Stamp the smaller stars in the same way.

Stamping the border mosaic

1 On to the larger block of wood, stick 12mm (1/2in) squares of foam stickers, leaving a space between each: the block will take nine stickers. Remove the second protective backing paper from each pad, before applying the paint.

2 Paint three squares on the stamp in each of the following colours: lilac, powder blue and fuschia. Prime the stamp as before, then press it around the perimeter of the rug, turning the stamp to give a different arrangement of colour. Reapply the paint between applications.

Stamping the central mosaics

1 Cut nine stickers into 10mm (3/8in) squares, then stick on to the smaller block of wood.

2 Using pale blue, duck egg blue, lemon/white, fuschia/white and turquoise/white, paint the foam stickers on the stamp; prime, then press firmly on to the rug. Reapply fresh paint after each application, so that the colours are printed evenly. Work across the background of the rug turning the stamp occasionally.

3 When the stamp is to be applied where it will overlap another stamped area, mask off the already stamped area with paper. The stamp will print on the paper and in the places not covered by the paper. Complete the background in this way, then allow to dry.

Sealing the mosaic rug

1 To protect the rug from wear, brush several coats of PVA glue mixed with an equal quantity of water over the rug. Allow to dry completely between each coat.

Applying the mosaic look

1 Dimensional finisher will give the mosaic tiles a three-dimensional appearance but should not be used in areas of high traffic. Beginning at the centre and working outwards, squeeze a line of dimensional finisher just inside each stamped mosaic tile shape. Fill the centre of each and allow the finisher to run out to the edges. Leave to dry overnight.

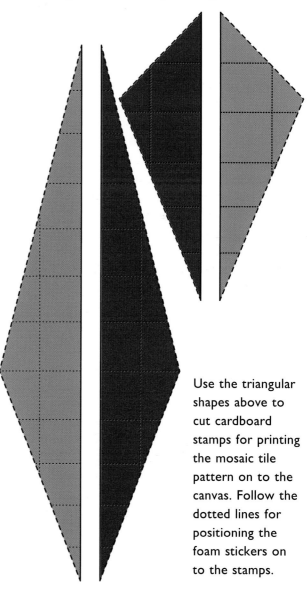

Use the triangular shapes above to cut cardboard stamps for printing the mosaic tile pattern on to the canvas. Follow the dotted lines for positioning the foam stickers on to the stamps.

Fish and Shell Paper Mosaic

Use this quick and easy method to create a mock mosaic look on plain dinner plates. The mosaic pieces, cut from decorative papers, use a simple découpage technique to give them a three-dimensional look. So, in just a few hours you can have a display of decorated plates on your shelf or dresser

Old ceramic plates can be used to complete this project: spray the back and front of the plate with a coat of cellulose primer and then two coats of cellulose paint.
NOTE: The decorated plates should be used for decorative purposes only.

You will need
- 24cm (9½in) diameter plates
- Scraps of giftwrap and wallpaper
- Découpage finisher
- Dimensional finisher
- Paintbrush, decorator's paintbrush
- White paper, soft pencil, chinagraph pencil
- Soft cloth, kitchen paper, cocktail stick

Transferring the design

1 Wash the plates in warm soapy water and dry thoroughly.

2 Lay white paper over the fish, shell and starfish motifs on pages 51, 52 and 53. Trace the designs carefully using a soft pencil. You can use a photocopier if you would prefer not to mark your book or if you need to enlarge or reduce the size of the motifs to fit the plate.

3 Cut out the tracings, then position one of the tracings centrally on to a plate. Using a chinagraph pencil, draw around the tracing to transfer the design on to the plate. Mark the detail lines in freehand; alternatively, cut up the tracing on the detail lines and draw around the pieces.

Placing the pieces

1 Cut the giftwrap and wallpaper into random mosaic shapes, to represent broken china. Papers with a texture and those with an overall mottled pattern work best for piecing.

2 Position the paper pieces on the plate, leaving approximately 3mm (⅛in) between the pieces and the different design areas on the plate. Cut shaped pieces as you work, fitting them into the difficult corners and smaller areas of the design.

Piecing the fish plate

1 The fish is worked on a yellow plate: mix together salmon, orange, red and pink coloured paper for the fish's head and tail; white paper for the eye with a dark grey 'eye ball' on top; light grey for the mouth; and orange for the fin.

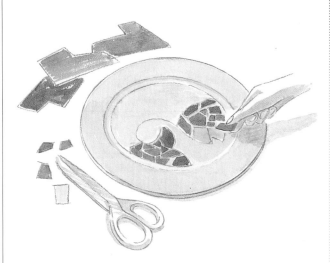

2 For the body use two shades of light green paper mixed with a few smaller pieces of light mauve.

3 Work the background around the fish in shades of bright blue.

4 The rim is worked in yellow paper, with a few pieces of darker orange and mauve.

Piecing the starfish plate

1 The starfish is worked on a blue plate, using yellow and orange.

2 Work the background in shades of bright green paper; and the rim in shades of blue, with a few pieces of orange.

Piecing the shell plate

1 The shell is worked on a green plate in sections, using shades of blue, pale blue and sea green paper in alternate stripes.

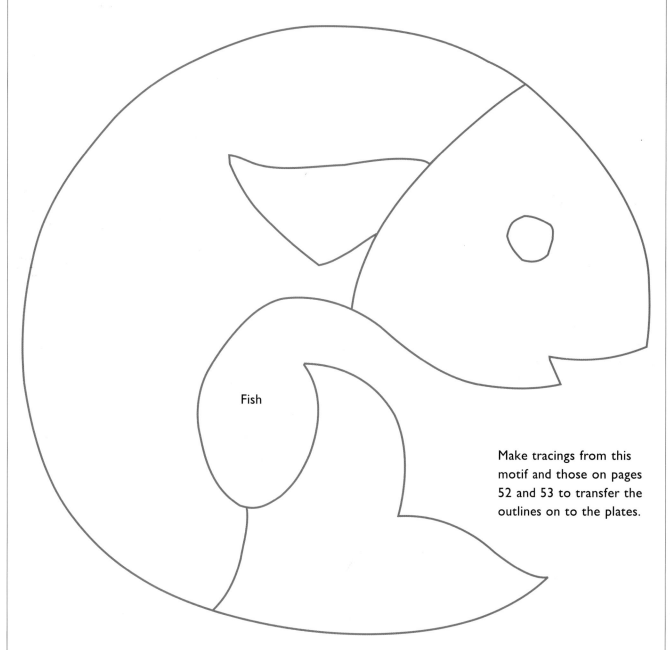

Fish

Make tracings from this
motif and those on pages
52 and 53 to transfer the
outlines on to the plates.

2 Work the background in shades of yellow
and pale orange paper; and the rim in
bright green, with a few pieces of orange and
yellow mixed in.

Fixing the pieces

1 Starting at the centre of the plate, stick the
mosaic pieces in place using découpage
finisher. Lift off one piece of paper at a time,

then, using a paintbrush, apply a coat of
finisher to the back of the paper (see Painting
Techniques, page 11). Re-position the paper
piece on to the plate, then, using your fingers,
smooth out each paper shape to remove the air
bubbles while spreading the excess finisher out
to the edges of the paper. Wipe off any excess
finisher with a soft cloth. Leave the plate to dry
for about 30 minutes.

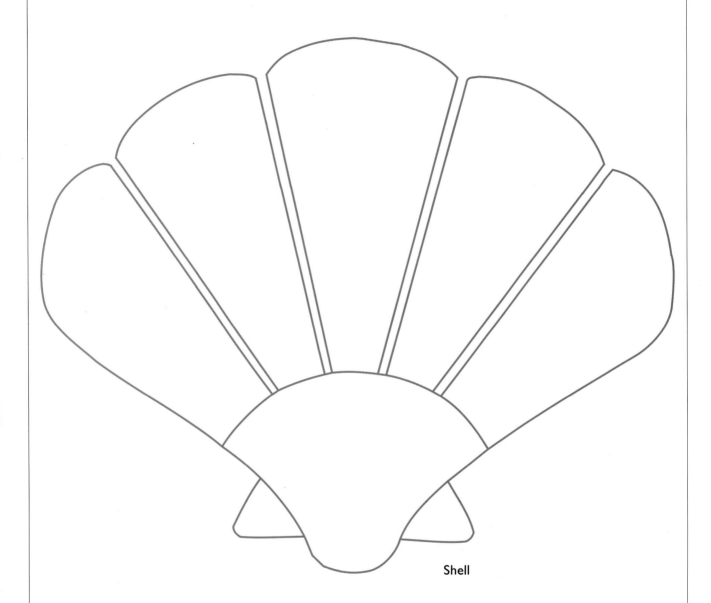

Shell

Finishing the plate

1 Using a decorator's paintbrush, apply a coat of découpage finisher over the front and back of the plate. Repeat after 20 minutes, then leave to dry for 20 minutes.

2 To give the paper mosaic pieces a three-dimensional look, they need to be coated with dimensional finisher to give them a raised finish. Great care should be taken when using dimensional finisher; it is a clear, runny liquid that will spread quickly on paper, if not checked. Starting on a paper mosaic piece close to the centre of the plate, squeeze the dimensional finisher very gently as you draw a line of liquid just inside the edge of the paper.

Starfish

Use a cocktail stick or cotton bud to take away any finisher that has run beyond the edge of the paper. Outline all the pieces in this way.

3 Leave the finisher to dry for a few minutes, then carefully squeeze a small amount of liquid into the centre of an outlined piece: allow the liquid to flow out to the edges.

Remove any finisher that runs over the outline, using a cocktail stick or cotton bud. Finish all the paper pieces in the same way, then leave to dry for at least three hours.

4 The plate should be used for decorative purposes only. To clean, wipe over with a dry cloth to remove dust.

Stylish Tray and Box

This stylish tray and box made from broken tiles is easy to complete in just a few evenings. Black, terracotta, orange and white tiles have been broken and then used to decorate a plain wooden tray and box. No specialist equipment is needed, just a hammer and brute force!

You will need

- Wooden tray, cardboard box with lid
- Thin tiles – terracotta, orange, black, white, fawn, stone
- Ready-mix tile adhesive
- Mosaic grouting
- Raw umber powder or acrylic paint
- Hammer, old tea towel, goggles
- Sheet of plastic bag
- Old cutting board or wooden off-cut
- Pencil, ruler, palette knife, sponge
- One container for each coloured tile
- Small paintbrush, bowl of water
- Emulsion paint – black
- Acrylic varnish

Planning the design

1 Sand the surface of the tray, then wipe off any dust with a damp cloth.

2 Following the photograph opposite, mark the position of the black curved band diagonally across the tray. Check that it extends an equal distance from each corner.

Preparing the tiles

1 It is advisable to wear goggles to protect your eyes when breaking the tiles. Wrap the black tile in the old tea towel and, on the wooden board, break it into small pieces with a hammer.

2 When you unwrap the tile, you will find some of the pieces are still too large. Place the plastic bag over the pieces so you can see them and break each one with the hammer into pieces that are no larger than 1cm (³/₈in) across.

Tiling the tray

1 With the small paintbrush, apply a thick layer of tile adhesive over the curved band on the tray.

2 Spread out the pieces of black tile near the tray; this will make it easier to choose the right piece for each space, rather like completing a jigsaw puzzle.

3 When the adhesive on the tray has dried to just tacky, apply more adhesive to the bottom of each piece of tile before you place them on the tray. Work along the curved band until it is completed. If the adhesive on the tray dries, add more and allow to go tacky before sticking the tile pieces down.

4 Break up the other tiles in the same way, then sort the different colours into separate containers.

5 To position the small square in the centre of one of the halves, measure up and across an equal distance from the tray sides, approximately 4cm (2in). Find four pieces of fawn mosaic with squarish edges to make a square; glue the pieces in place.

6 Brush adhesive over the rest of this half of the design. Lay out the orange and terracotta pieces ready for use.

7 Work with the two colours together, mixing them to fill one side of the tray around the fawn square.

8 Make a small square on the other half, with four pieces of orange tile. Apply adhesive to

the tray and then, using fawn, white and stone coloured pieces, fill the remainder of the tray.

9 Leave to dry for at least 24 hours before grouting.

Grouting the tray

1 Mix grouting with enough raw umber powder to make an oatmeal colour. Stir in sufficient water to make a sloppy mix. Alternatively, mix the grout with water and then add a little raw umber acrylic artists' paint to the mix.

2 With a palette knife, spread the grout over the tray, pushing it well into the cracks.

3 Wipe the tray with a damp cloth several times to remove the excess grout. Leave to dry for 24 hours, then wipe over again. Buff with a soft cloth to make the tiles shine.

4 Paint the sides of the tray with black emulsion paint.

5 When dry, varnish the painted sides with acrylic varnish. Do not varnish the mosaic.

Covering the box

1 Using a pencil and ruler, and following the photograph above for position, draw a large and a small square on the lid of the box.

2 Using the same method as described for the tray, attach two squares of terracotta tiles to the box top. Fill the surrounding area with a mixture of fawn, white and stone tile pieces.

3 For the lid sides, fix a row of black tile pieces around the top edge, with terracotta pieces beneath. Try to select pieces with straight edges as this will give the box a neater finish.

4 Fill the lower part of the lid sides with paler pieces. Leave the box to dry for 24 hours.

Grouting the box

1 Mix the grout in the same way as for the tray, then spread the grout over the box top. Make a neat edge at the corners and along the bottom by running your finger along the wet grouting. Leave to dry for 24 hours.

2 Paint the box, inside and out, with black emulsion paint. Paint a black line around the top and bottom edges of the lid.

3 When dry, varnish the painted areas with acrylic varnish. To clean the tray and box top, wipe over with a damp sponge, then buff to a shine with a soft cloth.

Wood Mosaic Bird Tables

Pre-cut balsa-wood shapes have been used to create a mosaic pattern on this pretty bird table and nesting box. The shapes, which are readily available at most craft shops, can be painted or stained, and then glued in place before grouting

You will need

- Bird table and nesting box kits (available at most craft shops)
- Balsa-wood mosaic shapes
- Wood glue
- White paper, pencil
- Acrylic paint – cerise, orange, turquoise, royal blue, light blue, lilac, terracotta, yellow
- Paintbrushes
- Water-resistant varnish – clear
- Grout – white
- Rubber gloves, water
- Container for mixing grout

Choosing your design

1 Before you assemble the bird table or nesting box, decide where you will be applying the balsa-wood mosaic shapes. Lay the parts to be covered with mosaics on white paper (in this project it was the roofs) and draw around them with a pencil to produce a plan.

2 Lay the balsa-wood shapes on to the plan, and when you are happy with the arrangement, draw around each shape.

3 If you are covering a large area, mark a number on the back of each balsa-wood mosaic shape to correspond with a number on your plan. Try to arrange the shapes so that they fit together, leaving gaps between, but with no large gaps at the edges.

Assembling the bird table

1 Make up the wooden bird table or nesting box following the kit instructions; leave off any decoration that will obscure the area to be covered with the balsa-wood mosaic shapes.

Painting the shapes

1 Paint the wooden balsa-wood shapes on one side with two or three coats of acrylic paints, using a variety of colours; leave to dry between coats, then add a coat of clear water-resistant varnish to seal the paint.

Applying the wooden shapes

1 Paint the bird table or nesting box, with two or three coats of acrylic paint in the areas where the mosaic will not be applied; leave to dry for several hours. The bird table is painted in two shades of orange, and the nesting box in yellow with lavender and orange highlights.

2 With a medium paintbrush apply wood glue to the reverse side of a balsa-wood mosaic shape. Following your plan, press the piece firmly in place, holding for a few seconds until the glue starts to dry. Do not apply too much glue to the shape or it may seep out; wipe away any excess with a cloth. Repeat with the other pieces, until the area is covered.

3 The squares and triangles on the nesting box are painted in turquoise, green, blue, lavender, orange and yellow; and the hearts and triangles on the bird table are burgundy, yellow and two shades of orange.

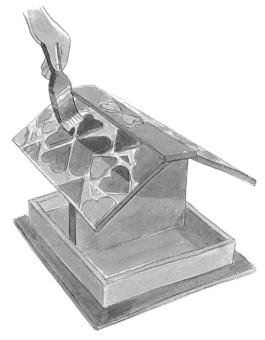

4 Paint the bird table or nesting box with a coat of water-resistant, clear varnish. The varnish must completely cover the wooden shapes or the grout will get under the pieces; leave to dry overnight before continuing.

Applying the grout

1 Mix the grout with water to form a fairly stiff paste.

2 Wearing rubber gloves, press the grout into the spaces between the painted shapes. Run your finger along the edges to create a smooth neat finish.

3 Before the grout dries, wipe over the wooden shapes with a damp cloth to remove excess grout. Rinse the cloth and repeat until all the grout is removed.

4 If the grout has marked the painted wooden pieces, they will need to be touched up with paint to remove the marks.

5 Paint the finished bird house or nesting box with two or three coats of clear waterproof varnish.

Cutting your own shapes

1 If you have trouble finding pre-cut wooden shapes, then you can cut your own from balsa-wood using the templates below.

2 Trace the shapes on to white paper, and then lay the paper templates on to 2mm (1/16in) craft balsa-wood (available from model shops). Draw over the shapes, transferring the design lines to the wood.

3 Lay the wood on a cutting board, then cut out the shapes using a craft knife.

Use these templates to cut your own balsa-wood mosaic shapes.

Acknowledgements

Thanks to the designers for contributing such wonderful projects:
Summer Dining (page 14), Lynn Strange
Eggshell Desk Set (page 22), Cheryl Owen
Magical Glass Vases (page 26), Jan Cox and John Underwood
Farmyard Placemats (page 30), Julie Cook
Seaside Mosaics (page 36), Martin Penny
Trug and Plant Holder (page 40), Susan Penny
Fabric-Painted Mosaic Rug (page 44), Lynn Strange
Fish and Shell Paper Mosaic (page 48), Cheryl Owen
Stylish Tray and Box (page 54), Kate Fox
Wood Mosaic Bird Tables (page 58), Jan Cox and John Underwood

Many thanks to Jon Stone for his inspirational photography;
Lakeland Limited for supplying the desk set; Paul Fricker for supplying
mosaic tesserae tiles and The Maritime Company for supplying props
used in photography.

Other books in the Made Easy series

Ceramic Painting (David & Charles, 1999)

Stamping (David & Charles, 1998)

Stencilling (David & Charles, 1998)

Glass Painting (David & Charles, 1998)

Silk Painting (David & Charles, 1998)

Suppliers

Craft World (Head office only)
No 8 North Street
Guildford
Surrey GU1 4AF
Tel: 07000 757070
Retail shops nationwide, telephone for local
store
(Craft warehouse)

Paul Fricker Ltd
Well Park
Willey's Avenue
Exeter
Devon EX2 8BE
Tel: 01392 278636
Mail order service
(Mosaic tiles, nippers, adhesives)

Hobby Crafts (Head office only)
River Court, Southern Sector
Bournemouth International Airport
Christchurch
Dorset BH23 6SE
Tel: 0800 272387 freephone
Retail shops nationwide, telephone for local
store
(Craft warehouse)

Homecrafts Direct
PO Box 38
Leicester LE1 9BU
Tel: 0116 251 3139
Mail order service
(Glass mosaics)

Lakeland Ltd
Alexandra Buildings
Windermere
Cumbria
LA23 1BQ
Tel: 01539 488100
Retail shops nationwide and mail order service
(Cardboard storage boxes)

The Maritime Company
Witney
Oxfordshire
OX8 6BH
Tel: 01993 770450
Mail order service
(Maritime gifts)

The Mosaic Workshop
Unit B
443-449 Holloway Road
London
N7 6LJ
Tel: 0171 263 2997
Mail order service
(Glass mosaics, equipment)

Edgar Udny & Co
The Mosaic Centre
314 Balham High Road
London
SW12
Tel: 0181 767 8181
Mail order service
(Mosaic tiles, nippers, adhesives)

Index

Page numbers in italics refer to main photograph

Acknowledgements, 62
Acrylic mosaic shapes, 26
Applying grout, 13, 17

Bird tables, 58
Box, 54
Broken china, 11
Buffing grout, 13

Cellulose primer, 7, 48
Cleaning grout, 13
Coasters, 30
Cutting glass tiles, 9, 10, 14
Cutting, Fixing and Piecing, 9–12

Découpage finisher, 11, 51, 52
Dimensional finisher, 52

Eggshell Desk Set, 12, 22–25, *23*
Epoxy glue, 12, 38

Fabric-Painted Mosaic Rug, 44–47, *45*
Farmyard Placemats, 30–35, *31*
Fish and Shell Paper Mosaic, 48–53, *49*
Fixing tiles, 10
Flower pot holder, 43
Flower pot, 18
Freehand design, 8

Glass pieces, 9
Grouting, 13

Introduction to Mosaics 6–7

Lamp, 38
Letter rack, 22

Magical Glass Vases, 26–29, *27*
Mixing grout, 13

Mock mosaic, stamping 12, 44, paper pieces 11, 48

Notepad, 24

Painting surfaces, 8
Paper-backed technique, 10
Pencil pot, 24
Placemats, 30
Plaster pieces, 9, 30
Plates, 48
Preparing Surfaces, 8
Protective equipment, 7
PVA glue, 8, 16

Rug, 44

Sealing surfaces, 8
Seaside Mosaics, 36–39, *37*
Shells, 36
Silicone glue, 9
Stamping, 12, 44
Step, 36
Stones, 12, 36
Stylish Tray and Box, 54–57, *55*
Summer Dining, 14–21, *15*
Suppliers, 63

Table top, 14
Tile backing paper, 10, 14
Tile nippers, 14
Tinting grout, 13
Tracing your design, 8
Transferring the design, 8
Tray, 54
Trug and Plant Holder, 40–43, *41*

Varnish, 18
Vases, 26

Wood Mosaic Bird Tables, 58–61, *59*
Wooden shapes, painting 12, applying 12

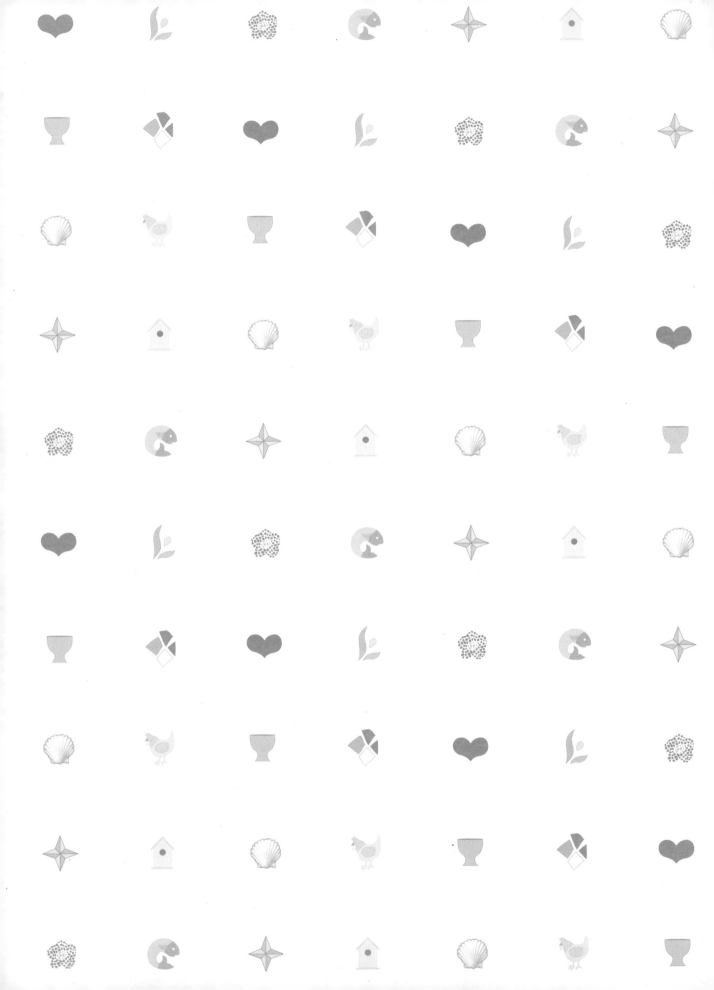